"Human Beasts" and Animals

₁₁ Daniel then said to the guard […]: ₁₂ "Test us for ten days: give us nothing but legumes to eat and water to drink, ₁₃ then compare our appearance with that of the young men who eat the food of the king" … ₁₄ So, he agreed to this and tested them for ten days; ₁₅ at the end of this time, everybody could see that their appearance was more beautiful and glowing than any of the young men who ate the food of the king …"

—Daniel, 1,11-15, *The Jerusalem Bible*

"Human Beasts" and Animals

Anna Pellanda

PARK PLACE PUBLICATIONS
Pacific Grove, California

English revised edition: May 2020
Print ISBN 978-1-943887-66-8
Park Place Publications, Pacific Grove, CA U.S.A.
www.parkplacepublications.com
© 2020 Anna Pellanda
All rights reserved.

Print and eBooks: available on-line at these locations:
United States: Amazon.com
Germany: Amazon.de
Spain: Amazon.es
France: Amazon.fr
Italy: Amazon.it
United Kingdom: Amazon.co.uk

First edition: March 2019
ISBN 978 88 5495 042 9
C.L.E.U.P. "Coop. Libraria Editrice Università di Padova" via G. Belzoni 118/3 - 35121 Padova (tel. +39 049 8753496) www.cleup.it - www.facebook.com/cleup

© 2019 Anna Pellanda
All rights of translation, reproduction and adaptation, total or partial, by any means (including photostatic photocopies and microfilms) are reserved.

CONTENTS

The Premise · 11
  What Men and Animals Have in Common
    Introduction · 13
    Suffering · 17
    The Language of Music · 22
    The Will to Live · 28

  What Sets Humans and Animals Apart
    Introduction · 33
    Seeking Economic Profit · 35
    The Demand of Food From Animal Origins · 41
    Cruelty and Ignorance · 46

  Q&A Session · 53
  Bibliography · 55
  Websites · 59

Addendum
  The Bat's Last Flight · 60

Thanks

This English translation of "*Umane belve*" *e animali* is due entirely to the generosity and the conviction of Professor Emeritus of Economics William D. Grampp of the University of Chicago and of Mrs. Annette Giganti. The belief in the aim of my survey and the approval of its content made them feel it deserved to be translated for circulation among English speakers. It is a marvelous reward for my efforts, and my gratitude is immense.

It contrasts with the silence I received from some friends and colleagues in Italy who even forgot to thank me for posting them a copy of the survey, and with the bureaucratic difficulties advanced by the University of Padova (the Rector being abroad), for denying its sponsorship during the first presentation of the work.

But not all is dark on this side of the Atlantic, and I wish to thank Professors "Emeriti": Salvatore Bartholini, Giovanni Maria Flick, Gilberto Muraro, and Paolo Zatti, for their important support in private correspondence, and Professor Cosimo Perrotta, for having published in his online magazine *Sviluppo Felice* parts of the survey. I am also grateful to the Associations: "Anziani a Casa Propria onlus", the Fondo Ambiente Italiano (FAI), the cultural Association "Serendo", the "Associazione Mazziniana Italiana" (AMI), the animalist Associations: AGIREORA EDIZIONI, CIWF, DINGO, ENPA, ESSERE ANIMALI, LAV, OIPA and – last but not least – the Municipality of Padua, which hosted and sponsored the first presentation of the treatise in June 2019.

To my parents who taught me the respect for animals, to Venice and to the Peloponnesian Doge for their love for cats, to the University of Padua for its lesson of *Universa Universis Patavina Libertas.*

The Premise

In the humans–animals relationship there are two questions that can be asked: are there any similarities between human beings and non-human beings, and what type of relation can be established between them?

In their uniqueness, humans must confront a group of animals with the most diverse characteristics, but it's mostly with mammals that they have to deal with. Of this relationship, studied in the past by philosophers, theologians and poets, there are different and often contradictory versions. With Darwin's research and with the progress of the natural sciences that followed, this relationship is analyzed from the perspectives of the response to equal suffering, of the musical language identity, and of the approach to life. The first part of this essay is dedicated to these three themes. The second part presents in depth the problem of the exploitation of animals, especially the use of them as food, although scientific research, clothing, hunting, circuses, and sports are well recollected in their own tragic reality. In the economy of today systems, the supply and demand of food of animal origins plays a fundamental role: the intensive farming of cattle, pigs, sheep, chickens, and also of fish represents the support structure of the production of international food corporations. The way they pursue profit, with the cruelest methods of industrial farming, is here denounced. This is matched with the demand of food of animal origins: gluttonous, pretentious, and completely deaf to animal suffering and to the nefarious consequences on human and environmental health of today's systems of production of food of animal origins.

The essay closes with a fierce description of the human cruelty that is unleashed in intensive farming and in the slaughterhouses where animals not only suffer immense pain but also have to face shameful human sadism. The individual human conscience has the responsibility to put an end to such barbarism.

What Men and Animals Have in Common

Introduction

In *Dei Sepolcri,* Foscolo writing: "When the day came when marriage, laws and altars/Gave to the human beasts respect/Both for themselves and others," he was sure that human beings evolve, can create legal works, and feel compassion for their and others' suffering. Unfortunately, that's not the case: humans continuously fall back into their tragic mistakes, such as wars, gender violence, and the destruction of the environment, and what they create is often only a hypocritical justification of economic, social, and even religious misdeeds. With the passing of time, humans have not detached themselves from the cave experience, but they have just wrapped it in a cloak of elaborate excuses to claim rights and not recognize their own duties, in order to impose their clever arrogance on those who have less chance to resist, thus addressing their supposedly evolved skills to the "evil object" (*Purgatorio*, XVII, 95). Humans are very dangerous beasts: grabbing, deceiving, and ruthless. Compared to them, animals, different in their core, seem driven only by natural survival instincts, pursued without duplicity, and with a dismal inability to resist human subjugation.

The animals vs. humans competition is unfair, but not for the superiority of one species over the others, but because of the regression of humans to savagery, disguised by civic duty. Humans exploit animals and call this economic law; they harass defenseless animals and define this practice as scientific experimentation; they make animals the target of hunting, circus farces, sports competition, and justify and decode them as their right to "happy" entertainment. Even in their need for God, they have generated beliefs that support their priority privilege, calling it "creationism" and denying any inferior evolutionary derivation.

To this economic-legal-theological structure, humans often add another layer, erroneously defined as "beastly": cruelty. The tortures that humans make animals suffer in intensive farming, in slaughterhouses, in bullfights, circuses, and in the world of sport, are committed by "banal" individuals, "without ideas," as Hannah Arendt defines them. As in the case of the criminals of the Holocaust, it's about men who are "neither perverse nor sadistic … rather terribly normal," whose circumstances "prevent them from realizing or feeling that they're acting badly."[1] They are men with no education, but certainly they are not animals, as often commonplace language would define them, because animals kill for hunger, hunt for survival, and do not torture. To animals, the sadistic dimension, the will to exploit, and the desire to humiliate, typical of humans, are unknown. The so-

---

1 Arendt, H., *Eichmann in Jerusalem*, New York, Lotte Kohler, 1963. Quotations from the Italian edition: *La banalità del male. Eichmann a Gerusalemme* (1963), Milano, Feltrinelli, XXVII ediz. 2016, p. 282. On the comparison between The Holocaust and the massacre of animals, see also Patterson, C., *Eternal Treblinka: Our Treatment of Animals and the Holocaust*, New York, Lantern Books, 2002.

called progress was used by humans to transform the original savagery into sophisticated manipulations at their own advantage. Only the artistic sensitivity can escape this destiny of perversion.

But what are the objective bases of the human/animal relationship? Does anything like ontological essence of coexistence, on Bettiol's[2] thought, really exist? To deeply analyze these concepts would mean to enter the realm of the metaphysical research of universal and necessary values, because we would enter the sphere of divine creationism vs. science evolutionism for the moment not penetrated. Instead we'll concentrate on the research for the objective grounds in which human/animal relationship finds incontrovertible collocation. We'll look for a substantial principle that demonstrates the regular kinship between humans and animals and the cruelty of human ferocity against their "little siblings." In the current state of scientific knowledge, this may only lie in the individuation of the natural characteristics that

---

2 Bettiol refers to S. Cotta's doctrine about human beings, according to which: "The two concepts 'respect for the innocents' and 'coexistence' should be implied both analytically (a priori) based on pure reason, and on facts (a posteriori) because: "The respect for the innocents is necessary not *only* for the individual existence…but it's necessary also for the *coexistence*. As soon as this respect fails…we have Hobbes' state of nature: *homo homini lupus*…so the respect for the innocents is necessary for the existence of human coexistence." This approach according to Bettiol is derived from the inductive method and the falsification of empirical sciences and she holds that it can help only the sphere of the factual "generality" and not of the "indisputability," detectable from the authentic "*ontological status,* that of the human person." The human person, according to Bettiol, has the "ability to distinguish good from evil" or his ontological goal. It's not necessary to underline that Cotta's concept of innocents, in this essay, is attributable to animals. See Bettiol, M., *Metafisica debole e razionalismo politico*, Napoli, ESI, 2002, pp. 194, 195, 196, 212.

legitimate the existence of the resemblance between humans and animals. These can be discerned in the concepts of "suffering" of Bentham fame, of "musical" language, recently studied by Genetics, and will end with an indication that seems undeniable, both from a natural and a teleological point of view, that is the right to life that humans and animals have in common and that imposes the respect for the other even if different.

Suffering

Theophrastus (372-287 B.C.) writes: "Children coming from the same origin, that is from the same father and from the same mother, we say that they are related by nature .... It's like saying, I think, of a Greek man in front of another Greek man, of a Barbarian in front of another Barbarian, of all men in front of the other men, who are related, part of the same race .... Similarly, we hold that all men, but also all animals, belong to the same ancestry, because ... the soul that is in them is not different by nature relatively to the desires, to the wrath, to the thought (*logismois*) and above all to the feelings. As for the bodies, some animals have a more or less perfect soul; but for all living beings, the principles are the same, by nature. The affinity of affection can prove it."[3]

In 1789 Jeremy Bentham writes: "One day, the rest of the animals will be able to acquire those rights that had been denied only by tyranny ... what else should draw the insuperable line? The ability to think, or that of language? But an adult horse or a dog are doubtlessly more rational and more communicative than a one-day, a one-week, or even a month-old baby. Even so, what would matter? The question is neither, 'Can they think? Nor 'Can they speak?' Rather the question is, 'Can they suffer?'"[4]

It is through suffering, the ability to have "feel-

---

3 Theophrastus, *Fragment X* in: Theophrastus, *Peri Eusebeias (About Pity)*, 316–315, Italian translation edited by Ditadi, G., *Della Pietá*, Este, Isonomia, 2005, pp. 261-263.
4 Bentham, J., *An Introduction to the Principles of Morals and Legislation* (1789), Oxford, Clarendon Press, 1966, ch. 17.

ings," as Theophrastus and Bentham point out, the natural and irrefutable common denominator, that connects humans to animals.

It's not surprising that Theophrastus was one thousand years ahead of Bentham, because great minds are typically ahead in time. But it's surprising that during that time[5] the question of animals and the object of finding a specific characteristic that would sanction their similarity was not addressed, as instead Bentham does. Before 1789, religious and secular thinkers' attention revolved only around the ability to think and to the legitimacy of animals' exploitation.

If we consider the attention that the Fathers and Doctors of the Church give to the animals issue, we see that it's been dominated by "the Jewish structure of the *Genesis* and ... the utilitarian concept of the use of animals .... The voices in favor of animals rise very sporadically and are in general considered heretic, such as those of the vegetarian Cathars or those of the mystics of Saint Victor .... Only rarely we can see figures who contrast superstition and religious obscurantism and strangely see pairs of nearly contemporary saints who oppose each other."[6] If Saint Ambrose, in his 387 *Hexaemeron*, denies animal rational thinking but not their "acute sensitivity," Saint

---

[5] Another ancient Greek philosopher interrupts this silence, Plutarchus I cent. A.D., (about whom we'll widely speak afterwards) who, in his two works *Moralia* and *De Esu Carnium* (*Of eating meat*), highlights the ability to feel and animals' moral courage.

[6] Pellanda, A., "Dalla venerazione religiosa allo sfruttamento economico" in *Noi e i diversi*, Atti del Convegno dell'Università di Padova, 12/02/1014, Padova University Press, 2014, pp. 26-27.

Augustine, in his 396-398 *Confessiones*, reiterates that humans have power over all animals. Almost one thousand years later, while Saint Francis in his 1224 *Canticum* celebrates the divine creation of all the creatures, Saint Thomas, in his 1265-1273 *Summa Theologica*, proposes again Aristoteles' concept of subordination of the inferior to the superior being, and the biblical concept of exploitation of the first one by the second one, "with the only danger that showing cruelty towards animals might be habit-forming and translate into cruelty towards humans."[7]

With regard to secular thinkers, they don't go beyond the hierarchical consideration on the reason/instinct contrast until, with Descartes, animals are completely assimilated into machines. In his most famous work, *Discours de la Méthode* (1637), Descartes doesn't deny animals' ability to have feelings, rather their ability to be able to communicate them through language and to be aware of them through thinking, as humans do. Animals are therefore mechanisms acting by instinct, without a soul, and this justifies human dominion on them.[8] Such a drastic position inspires Voltaire's reaction, who defines it (*Dictionnaire philosophique*, 1764), "a shame" and "a misery" while Rousseau, in his *Èmile* (1762), holds that humans and animals are similar by observing the intestines and the teeth of carnivorous and vegetarians; these last ones' teeth are "flat" like the teeth of not ferocious beasts and of humans who, since

---

7 *Idem*, p. 28.

8 Ditadi, G., edited by, *I filosofi e gli animali*, Torino, AgireOra Edizioni, 2010, pp. 154-159.

the beginning of time, have fed on vegetables only.[9]

Many philosophers from the 18th century until nowadays have thought about the humans/animals relationship, but the true successors of Bentham's thought are the Australian Peter Singer and the American Tom Regan and, still in the Anglo-Saxon world, the first contemporary works on animal suffering appear. These are *Silent Spring* by Rachel Carson, in 1962, and *Animal Machines* by Ruth Harrison, in 1964. Carson is "the first to denounce the dangers for food and the countryside ... caused by the continuous use of chemical products,"[10] and Harrison describes how farmers see in animals "only the factor of conversion into food for men."

"Intensive farming was born officially," Lymbery[11] comments. P. Singer[12], by examining the legitimacy of the behavior of humans towards animals, defines, for example, the experimentations on animals as abominable as those on humans[13] and the

---

9 Rousseau, J., *Èmile* (1762) in: Ditadi, G., *I filosofi e gli animali*, *op.cit.*, p. 202. Veronesi recalls this distinction in: Veronesi, U., Pappagallo, M., *Verso la scelta del vegetarismo. Il tumore si previene anche a tavola*, Milano, Giunti Editore, 2014.

10 Lymbery, P., Oakeshott, I., *Farmageddon. The True Cost of Cheap Meat*, London, Bloomsbury Publishing, 2014. Quotations from the Italian edition: *Farmageddon. Il vero prezzo della carne economica* (2014), Roma, Nutrimenti Srl, 2015, p. 9.

11 *Idem*, p. 13.

12 Singer, P., *Animal Liberation*, New York, Harper Collins Publishers, 1975.

13 *Idem*, pp. 73-74 on the experiments on Jewish, Russian and Polish prisoners by two hundred German doctors during the Nazi regime.

mentally disabled[14] because they all feel pain.[15] Tom Regan is the most decisive believer in animals rights; they must be protected not because they are useful to humans for their use and consumption, but in order to promote the animal's well-being (welfare) in itself, that is to say "in the true sense," to the point that it is simply unacceptable, for example, to make them suffer for experimental purposes.

It is evident how Bentham has opened a new school of thought that intends to contrast both the anthropocentrism of the Judeo-Christian faith and speciesism, the theory attributable to R. Ryder,[16] and based on the privileges granted to those who belong to a given species, excluding others. Both anthropocentrism and speciesism, the former a belief, the latter a theory, face the animal question trying a supporting, but diverse, foundation. The research for a principle that instead legitimates the kinship between animals and humans now considers the question of language, which was long discussed from different standpoints.

---

14 *Idem,* p. 75.

15 The scientific world too confirms that animals can suffer: see Menicali, S., *Introduzione al mondo animale*, ADIR-L'altro diritto, 2009, in particular chapter 2 and also the very rich bibliographic notes. See also Angelino, G.P., Raggioli, A., *Consapevolezza degli animali*, Roma, Aracne Editrice, 2018, in particular chapter 6 of Part II.

16 Ryder, R., *Victims of Science, The Use of Animals in Research*, London, Open Gate Press, 1983.

The Language of Music

Language is the means of communication that typically humans use, and it's considered their main tool to express and exchange thoughts: in some sense, it's reasoning uttered by voice. To make it simple: if we don't have reason, we can't speak.[17] Many, for a long time, have denied that animals have the ability to reason, with the premise that they don't speak because they don't have logical thoughts to express. According to this interpretation, animals simply emit sounds that don't have any intrinsically rational meaning, but in this way, we confuse the mechanism of the larynx with the prerogatives of the heart and the mind. The reality is that humans can't understand animals' calls, often not even those of pets.

The identification of language and reason, and for many also of language and soul, leads us to further analyze these concepts. If by reason we generally mean the ability to coordinate thoughts and to guide actions, on which we will return to, for the soul there are different concepts. In the Christian tradition, the most widespread one in the western world, the soul is created by God, it is immaterial, it guides matter/body and it is immortal. This simplification doesn't consider the different theories given by the Fathers and Doctors of the Church, the integrations of the different Councils and of the subsequent dogmas, nor the modern theologies that prefer to talk about "person" rather than soul. The common element in all these

---

[17] On the contrary, if one doesn't have a voice, because of any impairment, or if one is in the initial phase of life, one shouldn't be considered a reasoning being.

theses, we can say, is the divine derivation of the soul.

Descartes, the most decisive denier of the soul in animals, in turn, writes: "Besides, here I have gone into a detailed description of *soul*, because it's one of the most important topics; in fact after the mistake of those who deny God ... no mistake pushes weak spirits away from the righteous path of virtue more than thinking that the soul of the beasts is of the same nature as ours."[18] And, about language: "... even the deaf-mute are used to making up special signs to make themselves be understood," while "the reason why animals don't speak like us is not because they don't have the right organs, but because they don't have thoughts."[19]

This lack of kinship between humans and animals, due to the fact that animals neither have a soul, nor express themselves with words, as Descartes summarizes in a such a blunt and concise way, reflects the Christian philosophy and belief. If we went back in time, instead, we would see that the ancient Greek philosophy, from which all western thought begins, is characterized by very different points of view. Anaximander (VII cent. B.C.) for example, in his book *De Natura* holds that humans "come from animals of different species and that life originated from the sea."[20] His student, Pythagoras (VI cent. B.C.), and Empedocles (V cent. B.C.) hold that all

---

18 Descartes, R., *Discours de le Méthode* (1637), Part VI, passage quoted by Ditadi, G., *I filosofi e gli animali, op. cit.*, p. 155.

19 *Idem*, p. 158.

20 Anaximander in: Ditadi, G., *I filosofi e gli animali, op.cit.*, p. 65.

living creatures, including "word-less" animals, participate in the same nature and they all include a soul that transmigrates from one to the other, being reborn at each death; in fact, "there is one 'breath' that pervades the entire universe like a soul and makes us all one."[21]

If we considered the eastern philosophies and/or religions, we could see that the soul/language binomial is variously debated but also far from the western in both secular and religious thought. This analysis would require a separate study that's impossible here. Instead we choose to analyze the question of animal language by observing that sciences, most of all the neurosciences, hold that the gap between human and animal language should be revised after Darwin's lesson, who claimed that the difference between humans and animals is a matter of "degree and not genre" (Darwin, *The Origin of the Species*, 1859). From the working hypothesis that animal vocal expressions are complex but casual, neurosciences now recognize that the existence of universal congenital biological predispositions preside over both human language and the song of birds. Scientific studies concentrate on musical vocalizations of birds that show how they don't depend only on learning but rather on innate cerebral mental mechanisms, common to humans and animals.[22] From this cultural perspec-

---

21 Empedocles in: Ditadi, G., *I filosofi e gli animali, op. cit.*, pp. 71-72.

22 Logan, S.J., Sakata, J.T., "Vocal Motor Changes beyond the Sensitive Period for Song Plasticity," *Journal of Neurophysiology*, November 2014, pp. 2040-2052. See also Cimatti, F., *Mente e linguaggio negli animali. Introduzione alla zoosemiotica cognitiva*, Roma, Carrocci,

tive we examine the work of a musician who, with specific skills, studies this matter: Paolo Isotta's work on *Il Canto degli animali*.[23]

Isotta holds since the beginning of his research, that "not only music is linked by birth to animals: they are its cause, but also they taught it to us."[24] He starts from the concept of kinship between humans and animals that can be traced to ancient writing, such as Lucretius's (*De Rerum Natura*), Apuleius's (*Asinus Aureus*), Ovidius's (*Metamorphoses*), Vergilius's (*Georgica* and *Bucolica*), by which Giordano Bruno and Schopenhauer are inspired. Isotta highlights how the kinship between humans and animals, treated in literature and in poetry, is particularly evident in musical compositions. The main characters of this context are the lark, the nightingale, the swan, the hawk, the blackbird, the cicadas, and the frogs, described with an abundance of characteristics and meanings. He sums up his thesis by recounting a competition between a lute musician and a nightingale. The nightingale's song is described by Plinius with "extraordinary precision"[25] and inspires Gian Battista Marino who makes a reference to it and de-

---

1998, where the assonance and dissonance between human mind and language and animals' cognitive skills can be traced back from bees to chimpanzee. Also, Audet, J.N., Ducatez, S., Lefevre, L., "The Town Bird and the Country Bird," *Behavioral Ecology*, 2016, 27, pp. 637-644.

23 Isotta, P., *Il canto degli animali. I nostri fratelli e i loro sentimenti in musica e in poesia*, Venezia, Marsilio, 2017.

24 *Idem*, p. 31.

25 *Idem*, p. 217 and following.

velops it in his 1623 *Adone*[26] with the episode of the competition. The duet takes place in a wood where the musician sings his pain and the compassionate nightingale lands on his shoulder and imitates his melody. The musician is envious of it so he creates on his strings more and more difficult sounds. The nightingale accepts the challenge until his small being dies from exertion. The musician, admiring such courage and *bravura,* buries the nightingale in the cavity of his lute.

Isotta translates this competition into musical terms thus: "The musician, in order to obtain from his lute higher and higher pitched sounds, tunes it by turning the pegs and tightening the strings ('the nerves'); with the fingers of his left hand he goes as far down as possible, down to the "rose" (the sound hole), carved at the center of the belly to separate the strings. The nightingale, whether the instrument's sounds are high pitched or low (or, as it could be interpreted, the intonation lowers or raises the tuning fork pitch) weaves and mixes (*'implica e mesce'*) 'labyrinths of voice': its trills spread out so that they are compared to a labyrinth. The musician, taken by rage from the bird's resistance, puts all his efforts to find a new way of chanting ('to modify the verse') adding very fast passages ('quavers in fugue') and rhythmic shifts ('quavers askew/side crossing'). Three octaves are dedicated to the description of the unprecedented and unbelievable effects of his performance ....The hand flies on the strings more than the nightingale

---

26 Marino, G.B., *Adone* (1623), Canto settimo, secondo episodio, Milano, Adelphi, 1988.

itself can fly with his wings; the musician can 'inimitably imitate' with the sweetness of the melody 'the sweet songs'. The nightingale doesn't surrender but "At the end of the third octave" the small feathered creature dies from exhaustion.[27] If instead of an instrument we compared the nightingale song to human singing, their common musical virtuosos would be the same. Unfortunately, this symbiosis that seems to be based only on pure musical pleasure, in reality, except for in the arts, is used by humans to kill: humans imitate animal calls in order to attract, hunt or sacrifice them. Life taken from animals is the theme of what follows.

---

27 Isotta, P., *op. cit.*, p. 222.

The Will to Live

To the idle but frequent question asked to vegetarians and to vegans as to why they don't eat animals, the most obvious answer refers to the life that humans and animals share. Humans and mammals were born in the same way and they both want to live, as all the other animal species. But humans steal the life off of them as they take it from plants even if, as Theophrastus explains, "it's not the same kind of theft because it's not committed against ... the will (of the plants). Indeed, even if we don't touch them, they let their fruits fall; and picking their fruits does not entail the destruction of the plants as it happens for living beings when they lose their soul."[28]

Being alive means that nobody was born in order to be killed, nor exploited by others, but also that nobody was born to kill. Animals have the right to live and humans the duty to respect it. But humans disregard this duty even with regards to their kind when they send to war their young soldiers or when they kill women and, long ago, even slaves, or when they try to eliminate a race, for example the Jewish one, in the Holocaust.

Humans are capable of taking life, even their own, when it's too unbearable, while animals don't know suicide. Leopardi makes Plotinus say that "in nature

---

[28] Theophrastus, *About Pity*, op. cit., p. 130. Today vegetable neurobiology and one of its leading figures, Stefano Mancuso, hold that plants are not evolved, communicate among them only in order to survive but not to think; see Mancuso, S., *Plant revolution. Le piante hanno già inventato il nostro futuro*, Firenze, Giunti, 2017. The vegetal ethologist Jaques Tassin shares the same opinion, see Tassin, J., *Penser comme un arbre,* Paris, Odile Jacob, 2018.

suicide is not permitted: animals don't commit it."[29] Unfortunately, over time, group suicides of dolphins and whales have taken place; recently, on February 10, 2017, "four hundred whales, driven mad by noise pollution, went aground on the beach of Farewell Spit in New Zealand."

In 2018, one hundred specimens of pilot whales "lost their sense of direction" and were found stuck in sand on the beach of Hamelin Bay in Southwestern Australia while nine years ago eighty were stranded in the same bay. As many as one thousand lost their life a century ago in New Zealand.[30] It is indeed hypocritical to call these tragedies suicides. It's humans who, with their military training at sea and with deep sea oil drilling, damage cetaceous organs and drive them indeed to madness; they always remain together as these animals are extremely social and if they see an individual who, for any reason, heads for the beach, they don't abandon him, "they follow him even when this means to die."[31]

Humans not only kill animals, for example by hunting them for pleasure, but they also torture them in intensive livestock farming, in so-called scientific labs, in circuses, and in transportation systems (in general to slaughterhouses). Luckily, certain countries' legislation intervened to protect animal life that, though far from being as sacred as human life, must have some value. It's the problem of animal welfare, making its way from natural sciences and moving to-

---

29 Leopardi, G., "Dialogo di Plotino e di Porfirio" in: *Operette morali* (1835), Bari, Laterza, 1928, p. 199.
30 Isotta, P., *op. cit.*, p. 21.
31 Dusi, E., "Quelle balene soffocate dal legame di famiglia", *La Repubblica*, 24 marzo 2018. The number of stranding is alarming.

wards ethics, as the English Brambell Report of December 1965 shows; it sanctions the five fundamental freedoms (freedom from hunger or thirst; from discomfort; from pain, injury or disease; from unnatural situations; from fear and distress). This setting is adopted by the EU directive 63/2010/UE, aimed at improving, if not abolishing, animal experimentation and based on Russell & Burch's three 'R's':[32] "replacement, reduction, refinement" of use of animals. As Tallacchini[33] highlights, the problem that emerges more and more is that of the reciprocal influence between scientific knowledge about animals and the regulatory issues of legal systems; to these the researcher adds the "democratic" component, intended as empirical (factual) fundamental of ethics.

This combination of science and law presides over the initiatives of the international organizations that are committed to the improvement of animals' quality of life, such as OIE (World Organization for Animal Health), FAO, and WTO, when they provide recommendations and guidelines in favor of terrestrial and aquatic animals. Within a European context, there are two bodies, the Council of Europe and the European Commission, that are responsible for regulating the life mainly of pets[34] (the first) and mat-

---

32 Burch, R.L., Russell, W.L., *The Principles of Human Experimental Technique*, Wheathampstead, UFAW, 1992. See also Bono, G., De Mori, B., *Il confine superabile. Animali e qualità della vita,* Roma, Carrocci, 2011, pp. 48-56.

33 Tallacchini, M., "Dignità, etica science-based, democrazia: la tutela animale nella società europea della conoscenza" in: Chizzoniti, A.G., Tallacchini, M., edited by, *Cibo e religioni: diritto e diritti,* Roma, Libellula Editore, 2010, pp. 297-322.

34 *European Convention for the Protection of Pet Animals*, ETS 125, Strasburg, 13. XI. 1987.

ters related to economic matters mostly of the market and of consumers' health[35] (the second). However, the big problem within the EU is the discrepancy between European directives and their implementation by the national governments that have wide freedom of criteria in implementing, for example in matter of slaughter and experimentation.[36] Even the Treaty of Lisbon, of December 13, 2007, while definitively recognizing animals as sentient beings with the right to well-being, is not free from clashing with the legislations of the twenty-seven member countries.

This autonomy of the European countries is not always negative; for example, Germany has been the first country to include in its Constitution, on the 26th of July, 2002, animal protection and the prohibition of every abuse. Also in Italy the new wording of Art. 727 of the criminal code (Law 473, 1993) is an example of the shifting of the concept of animals as objects of compassion by humans to sentient beings worthy of well-being for their own natural identity. Law 281 of 1991 already protected pets and stray animals, and Law 189 of 2004 intervened in order to ban animal abuse and their use in illegal fights. Recently, legislative decrees have been enacted with the intent to improve the barbaric conditions in intensive farming, Law Decree 126 of the 7th of July, 2011, or animal suffering during experimentation, Law Decree 126 of the 4th of March, 2014. Unfortunately, in spite of national and regional laws, of legislative decrees

---

35 Tallacchini, M., "Gli animali nella Società Europea della conoscenza: contraddizioni e prospettive", Università Cattolica del Sacro Cuore and Piacenza, *PubliCatt.*, 2015, pp. 5-6.

36 *Idem*, pp. 9-10.

and ordinances in favor of the quality of animal life in farming, hunting, fishing and transportation, the condition of animals everywhere is far from being civil and respectful. The second part of this study is dedicated precisely to situations of human barbarization towards animals.

What Sets Humans and Animals Apart

Introduction

The first part of this study is focused on the foundations of the similarities between humans and animals, identified in suffering, language, and in the will to live. But, unfortunately, humans indeed deny animals the right to live. The second part of this study is so dedicated to the suppression of the life of animals by humans, accomplished for mere economic calculations, in order to satisfy gastronomic gluttony and social ambitions and to pour out the most inconceivable and unjustified inhumanity. As the thesis of the "I don't know" what is inflicted on animals is generally widespread, the most common atrocities will be described and informative websites will be given, for more information. In this way, the readers of this research won't be able to hide themselves behind a lack of information or resorting to "it's always been like this," or even to the raving accusations of ideological sectarianism directed to animalism. Reality can be brutal but never defaming, unless by deliberate cunning human misrepresentation.

Humans have peacefully lived with animals for a long time as witnessed by the Egyptian civilization where animals were the channel between humans and gods.[37] Humans used to eat only cereals and the fruits of the earth, as Ovidius claims, by saying

---

[37] Gardiner, A., *Egyptian Grammar* (1927), Oxford, Griffin Institute, 1957.

that only wild animals were killed in defense[38] and Theophrastus who holds that "hunger and wars ... brought up the necessity to eat animals."[39] But as long as there were crops enough for human livelihood, animals were not killed. Then, the hunting started and the killing of pets such as sheep and ox, the workmate of humans.[40] The killing of the ox, condemned by Pythagoras, Zarathustra, Theophrastus and Ovidius is the connection with the massacre of bovines, and also of pigs, sheep, hens, fishes, geese, fur and clothing animals in today's intensive farming. In such places there's no consideration for the animal who is a working mate and source of livelihood: he is killed in order to gain profits from complacent consumers. In fact, in front of our dishes there's no afterthought for the animal suffering that the food entails: animals are eaten only because of voracity, that's it. Therefore, here we reflect upon the supply and demand of animal foods. We will conclude by considering human cruelty towards animals of which we pretend of being unaware.

---

38 Ovidius, *Metamorphoses*, XV, 139-142 in: Theophrastus, *About Pity, op. cit.*, pp. 76-77.

39 Theophrastus, *About Pity, op. cit., Fragment* I=II, 5, 1, pp. 198-199.

40 See Ovidius in: Theophrastus, *About Pity, op. cit.*, p. 77, where we read: "Do not do this, please/listen to my warnings,/and when you offer the palate the limbs of slaughtered oxen,/know and let it be clear that,/you're eating our workers."

Seeking Economic Profit

Profit, understood as earnings of the entrepreneur after the production's costs ("residual profit"), has always had to defend itself from market competition, generally leveraging on the big dimension that practices low prices ("predators' prices"), trouncing small producers or obtaining legal concessions that allow monopolistic forms of production and sale of the products. Among the cattle farmers, and not only, the dilemma has always been: big or protected. Nowadays the intensive farming of boundless dimensions, and protected by anti-competition legislation, have both these attributes. In the United States, these kinds of characteristics have the face of ten multi-national corporations of meat, the "ten sisters of the agri-food system": ABF, Coca-Cola, Danon, G.M., Kellogg's, Mars, Mondolez, Nestlé, PepsiCo. and Uniliver.

Also intensive farming was born in the United States when, in Chicago, during the 1860s-1870s, the assembly line for slaughter houses was invented, with conveyor belts and cold storage rooms for the movement of the slaughtered animals.[41] It is here that: "In the big chain of life, bovines had been further downgraded: desecrated, as well as dis-

---

[41] Rifkin, J., *Beyond Beef. The Rise and Fall of the Cattle Culture* (1992). Quotations from the Italian edition: *Ecocidio. Ascesa e caduta della cultura della carne*, Milano, Mondadori 2001, pp. 136-143. Rifkin traces the history of these technological innovations put in place between Detroit and Chicago by the five greatest meat entrepreneurs: Hammond, Swift, the two Armor, and Morris, pp. 131-135. Chicago slaughterhouses inspired Henry Ford when he introduced the assembly line for the construction of his cars. As he recalls: "The idea came to us in general from the trolleys on tracks that Chicago butchers use to distribute the parts of the steer." Ford, H., *My Life and Work* (1922); (with Crowther), New York, Doubleday Page & Company, 1926.

membered, this icon of supernatural fertility was changed into a standardized factor of production by the high priests of efficiency—Gustavus Swift, Philip Armour, and all the others."[42]

In intensive farming, animals are as machines to be exploited as intensively as possible. It seems like the culmination of the Descartes' thesis of the animals without a soul, the gear of a machine that is useful to humans only. The economic theory translates this vision in technical terms using the cost/benefit analysis, the fundamental concept of which lies in the biggest reduction of costs to obtain the highest possible benefits. These goals are reached by leveraging economies of scale that are based on the large dimension and on technical progress. In reality, the boundlessness of intensive farming is made possible by using endless warehouses where thousands of animals are heaped in such crammed spaces that they can barely stand, but where (encouraged by strong lights that simulate daylight) they have to continuously eat, thus gaining weight and producing "income meat." In such places there's no air, no natural light, and the cattle litter is made of excrements and is the cause of sores and infections. Calves, taken away from their mothers after three or four days from their birth, in the first farms were kept in such barbaric conditions that convinced the European Commission to take action to improve them, at least partly.[43]

42 Rifkin, J., *op. cit.*, p. 138.

43 Community regulations 91/629 EEC and 97/2/CE and legislative decree 7/7/2011, 126, art. 6; see Cozzi, G., Gottardo, F., "Il nuovo sistema di allevamento del vitello a carne bianca" in *Atti della Società Italiana di Buiatria*, vol. 37, 2005, pp. 441-454.

Other examples of intensive farming involve pigs, sheep, fish, and chickens. Considering chicken farming, we must note that the big dimension allows keeping even tens of thousands of animals in the dark and in spaces of the size of a sheet of A4 paper per animal (that is 17 or 22 chickens per square meter). The litters are not changed and they soak in the ammonia of the excrements causing skin infections, painful leg deformities and even paralysis. Unable to move to the trough, some die of starvation or of thirst. The slaughter takes place after 38-40 days from the birth, or as soon as they reach the right weight. These conditions produce food-borne diseases caused by such bacteria as salmonellosis, Campylobacter infections, and even avian flu.[44] These horrible conditions cause stress and aggression among chickens to the point that they cut their beaks off with no anesthesia (see the following paragraph). Likewise, they cut the tails off pigs so they don't hurt themselves.

As far as technical progress is concerned, on which the costs/benefits analysis and its practical application have also been based in intensive farming, after the big innovations of Chicago during the 19th century, there are no important technical changes besides mechanical milking and distribution of feed on the conveyor belts of the troughs. This doesn't mean that technology is not used, because it is indispensable in order to reduce the average costs of production,[45] but it's used in another capacity: the

44 CIWF website: http://www.ciwf.it/animali/polli-da-carne//allevamento-intensivo.

45 The more mechanized livestock farming is, the fewer workers have to be employed and paid. It seems that one worker is enough to "tend to" a hundred chickens. Data on wages, schedules and jobs for both intensive farms and slaughterhouse workers are difficult to find.

pharmaceutical one. Pharmaceuticals in intensive farming are indispensable because, given that the ultimate goal is fattening the animals very quickly, growth promoting hormones are given and, because of animals' promiscuity, it's possible that it causes the contagion of infections and diseases, which are treated with more and more powerful antibiotics. Technical progress in intensive farming means pharmaceutical progress and scientific research; this is such that in Israel they have been able to create poultry without feathers to save space in cages and spare the plucking, while in the United States the cloning of chickens is already happening, and they're sold as safe food in supermarkets.[46]

The big dimension and technical progress both can lower the economic costs of the intensive farming, but not the social ones. This is the problem of the so-called inside and outside diseconomies; the inside ones consist of the terrible life conditions in which animals and workers are forced; the animals, as we have just seen, are stuffed with drugs and abused in their natural way of living, while workers, generally with no qualification, are recruited among "illegal immigrants" or "just migrated desperate" workers, and are badly paid (max. 8 euros per hour), and are liable for immediate dismissal if they protest or ask for the observance of their legal rights. Foer denounces that "the systemic violations of human rights often induce the responsible ones to vent their frustration

---

[46] Lymbery, P., Oakeshott, I., *Farmageddon, op.cit.* Quotations from the Italian edition: *Il vero prezzo della carne economica, op. cit.,* pp. 334-336, 340-341.

on the animals …. Some are clearly sadistic, in the literal sense of the term."[47] On this theme we'll return further on.

To these internal diseconomies are connected the external ones that fall back onto the environment and human health. The air and the water are in fact polluted by animals' emissions and excretions. FAO calculates that animal farming causes 60% of the emission of ammonia. In turn, animals' excretions are not disposed of, as it used to happen through grazing land, but are carried by conveyors into stagnant pools outside of the warehouses, then release nitrogen and phosphorous into the rivers and seas that they can reach, especially when it rains. The greenhouse effect and acid rains can be traced back to intensive farming, and also deforestation can be due to it. In Brazil, they destroy the Amazon rain forest at a frightful pace, and in Argentina every year they raze to the ground 200.000 hectares of forest to make space for soy crops and palm oil that represent the most common feed of the animals shut in the warehouses. As these crop productions are infested with parasites, the use of pesticides and herbicides is highly widespread. Even if soy, chemically treated, could feed entire malnourished populations, (more than one billion in the world), instead it's given to animals who don't have pasture or forage grasses.

This farming system allows few oligopolists to make very high profit, besides displaying the big hy-

---

[47] Foer, J.S., *Eating Animals,* New York, Little, Brown and Company, 2009. Quotations from the Italian edition: *Se niente importa*, Parma, Guanda Editore, 2013, pp. 114-115, 248, 272.

pocrisy of selling it at a low price to benefit consumers. The economic price is low, but the social one is very high, as we have seen. So far, we have indicated how it is possible for intensive farms to produce at low costs with the economies of scale, that is through the exploitation of animals and workers, and with pharmaceutical progress (with complete disinterest for environmental pollution and risks for human health), while at the same time making high profit. But do high profits have also another source? The answer comes from consumers and from the "positive" elasticity of their demand for meat.

The Demand of Food From Animal Origins

When Petronius, in the middle of the first century A.D. in his *Satyricon*, describes Trimalchio's dinner, based on eggs, hens, sausages, and different delicacies, he passes down an imperishable document on the social importance attributed to omnivorous diet. Trimalchio is a slave who has become a freedman and wants to show the Roman society of his time his new social status by astonishing it, in his Pompei house, with monumental banquets.

Nowadays, consumers keep matching food to the same sense of having reached the material wealth achieved with their social climbing. There are various confirmations of this relationship. From Rifkin, for example, we know how much importance to meat was given by the English. He speaks even of the "obsession" of the British for meat, dating back to pre-Christian Celts, inherited from feudal nobility and landowners, and culminating in the connection of colonial powers with the consumption of "fatty" meats, a symbol of opulence and imperialism. Rifkin writes: "In medieval England, aristocrats dissipated fortunes, time and energy to prepare elaborate meat banquets, in constant competition to surpass each other. In privileged classes, food and its preparation became instruments of crucial importance to show social class and privilege" and while the rich stuffed themselves with meat, the poor, practically excluded from meat diet until the middle of the nineteenth century, had to settle for what the English call 'white meat': cheese, milk, butter and other dairy products. Between the rich and the poor there were a more and more numerous working class and a wealthy and powerful middle class that strived to reach the meat habits of the nobility."[48]

The two historical examples mentioned before, far apart in time but equal in meaning, highlight the constant seeking of social status that is achieved through meat consumption, and also the greed below it. These two characteristics partly complicate the economic theory (marginalist) of the demand set up on the relation between needs and goods defined as utility. This relation, studied by Gossen in 1854,[49] and mathematically defined by Jevons in 1871,[50] becomes law, stipulating that the need decreases to its satisfaction, if satisfied with continuity, uninterruptedly and frequently. This means that utility is decreasing, and that the price the consumer is willing to pay consequently for a useful good (meat for example) used to satisfy his need (for meat food), is more and more decreasing. As Marshall establishes in 1890: "the quantity requested raises as prices go down and decreases as prices go up." This law applies both to individuals and to society because "the variety and the instability of individual actions diminish in the relatively regular aggregate of the action of many."[51]

---

48 Rifkin, J., *Beyond Beef, op. cit.*, pp. 66-67, 68.

49 Gossen, H.H., *Entwicklung der Gesetze des menschlichen Verkers* (1854), Berlin, Braunschweig, 1854.

50 Jevons, S.W., *Theory of Political Economy* (1871), London, MacMillan, 1871.

51 Marshall, A., *Principles of Economics* (1890), London, Bloomsbury Publishing, 2014, pp. 98-99.

In the specific case of the today's meat demand, people buy more if the price descends, the typical case of elasticity of demand, but at the same time, satisfaction is never achieved. The current consumption of meat, already considerable all over the world, is destined to grow because all the emerging countries including China[52] are increasing consumption. In reality, we witness the presence of low prices and high profits for producers.

This mechanism clearly deviates from Gossen's and Marshall's economic laws and requires a socio-psychological explanation that only institutionalist theories, from Veblen's[53] onwards, can provide: in fact, meat, a prime provision, is requested not only for individuals' need but also for the prestige that it conveys and for the voracity of the consumers. The need to consume meat as prime good for carnivores turned into compulsive use of meat as status symbol and into the refusal to change patterns of consumption, despite damages to the health, cruelty to animals and destruction of the environment. The demand for meat, with its "dimension," so offers strong support to the pursuit of profit for farmers. These, in turn, promote every form of publicity on the virtues of meat, disregarding the warnings of the harmful effects of its consumption on human health and completely deaf

---

52 In China, where every citizen eats 88 pounds of meat every year, the WH Group, after taking over the American Smithfield, has become the first producer in the world of products from pigs (*La Repubblica*, 17 maggio 2018).

53 Veblen, T., *The Theory of the Leisure Class* (1899), London, Allen & Unwin, 1924.

to the nefarious environmental consequences of its intensive production. In Italy, on November 21, 2018, an ASSOCARNI's ad was broadcasted, produced by RAI Pubblicità, as "Lessons of Label" and sponsored by the Ministry of Agricultural, Food and Forestry Policies (MIPAAFT) that, forgetful of being an institution that functions thanks to the taxes of all the citizens and therefore with the obligation to be impartial in front of the particular groups of consumers, instead celebrated the characteristics of a meat diet. All these initiatives leverage on the sociological and psychological reasons supporting the consumption of meat and fattening the profit of the producers. And habits, which much of today's economic theories investigate, are of conventional origins and die hard, once acquired. Plutarchus wrote that, "it is not easy to move men back from a wrong habit already turned into mechanical habit. The habit has in the majority of people the strength to influence (if not to determine) their intellect. The habit has the strength of a magic filter in generating vice and injustice" and although "man is not carnivorous by nature because he has no hooked beak, has no pointed claws, no robust stomach, has no warm humors capable of digesting and assimilating the heavy meat," in order to cultivate his carnivorous taste he changes and attenuates the taste of the blood of dead animals that he eats "with countless toppings because with the taste deceived, he can accept what by nature is alien to him," "We … who name meat 'delicacy', we can afford to stain ourselves with blood and then, for that same meat, in a refined way, we need toppings, mixing oil, wine, honey, cloves, vinegar with Syrian and Arab sauces, as if really we were preparing a corpse for burial."[54] In return, a modern author studies this issue more deeply, observing "a sort of moral schizophrenia, inducing us to take good care of our pets and at the same time not stopping us from sticking the fork into the meat of pigs, sent to slaughterhouses in millions; but they are as conscious, sensitive to pain and intelligent as our dogs and cats." The same kind of deafness is inherent in fur wearing, in experimenting in labs, in hunting because, "We live in the ignorance of what we inflict on animals."[55] The following section intends to help to defeat exactly this ignorance.

---

[54] Plutarchus, *De esu carnium (Of Eating Meat)*, quotations from the Italian translation edited by Ditali, G., *Sul mangiar carne*, Torino, AgireOra Edizioni, 2016, pp. 72-73.

[55] Ricard, M., *Plaidoyer pour les animaux*, Paris, Allary Editions, 2014. Quotations from the Italian edition: *Sei un animale. Perchè abbiamo bisogno di una RIVOLUZIONE ANIMALISTA* (2014), Trento, Sperling & Kupfer Editori, 2016, p. 4.

Cruelty and Ignorance

In this last section we address the problem of ignorance, of how humans do harm animals with the aggravating circumstances of unnecessary cruelty. In fact, not only do humans keep animals in horrific conditions in intensive farming, not only do they experiment with very painful practices in so-called scientific labs, but they also kill them in unnecessarily cruel ways in the slaughterhouses, fur industry and so on. Where does such brutality come from? Does the quoted thesis of the "banality" of evil by H. Arendt give a sufficiently exhaustive answer to the problem? Or is the dilemma, between obfuscation of moral conscience or a complete lack of conscience and respect, still unsolved for some individuals? Both alternatives belong to actions and thoughts that are shameful to humans: in the first case because human decay is the result of serious social non-fulfillments and/or psychological disorders, in the second because we support a moral hierarchy that discriminates against human beings from birth, bordering on racism.

In the places where animals are tortured and where they are atrociously killed, some people work there because they cannot find another occupation and/or are suffering from sadistic impulses as Foer denounces (see above). We can easily speak of socio-economical systems that cannot offer decent possibilities of work and care. In these contexts, the cruelty against animals would be a reaction to the bad luck in work and health taken out on defenseless beings. Anyhow, it's difficult to avoid the question of why such human cruelty exists. God himself, who saw "that the wickedness of man was great in the earth" (*Genesis* 6, 5), "regretted that he had made man" (*Genesis* 6, 6).

It's therefore time to witness, following Matthieu Ricard's book, what animals suffer at the hands of humans in a "system of torture and murder that is cruel, fast, efficient and profit oriented,"[56] and supported by social ambitions and human gluttony. As Ricard introduces, "What I'm going to describe to you is shocking. Perhaps should I precede it saying 'Beware! Could this content shock the most sensitive people?' However, in order to be able to genuinely feel involved in the fate of other beings, and therefore to act, as far as possible, so as to alleviate their sufferings, is it not necessary to gain awareness of them? History has shown us that looking away has always left free rein to the worst atrocities" (Ricard, p. 80).

According to FAO's statistics, 60 billions terrestrial animals are killed every year, "and more than 100 billions, according to other estimates" (Faostat.fao.org). One of the first documents on this massacre can be traced back to 1906, when the number of slaughtered beasts was, however, lower, and it's due to Upton Sinclair who describes Chicago slaughterhouses in his book *The Jungle*.[57] But we owe Jonathan Foer too the courage to have gone to these places, of difficult or even no access, to write *Eating Animals*

---

[56] Ricard, M., *op. cit.*, p. 85. From now onwards various passages from this work will be quoted because it is important to refer to a not disputable documentation or attributable to the imagination of animalists or even satanic extremists.

[57] Sinclair, U., *The Jungle*, New York, Doubleday, 1906.

with fearless reports.[58] Quoting from Ricard, who in turn follows Sinclair, we know what happens to pigs: "Some groups of pigs were pushed towards the chutes, sort of walkways as wide as a road …. Against the back wall was a large metal wheel, with a circumference of more than six meters, with a series of rings fixed to the hem with regular intervals …. The men on either side fastened the paw of the closest pig to a chain, hooking the other paw to one of the rings of the wheel, so that as soon as it moved, the pig was suddenly lifted from the ground and struggled in mid-air … a double row of pigs hung by one leg, kicking and grunting in despair, was made up …. As for men, the screeching of the pigs or the tears of visitors made no difference to them: they hooked the pigs one after the other and slaughtered them with a quick knife … the pigs emitted the last cries along with gushing of blood." (Ricard, pp. 84-85).

In a cattle slaughterhouse, the animals were brought into a corridor, "imprisoned in separate compartments" and kept very tight. "They bellowed and banged against the walls, while those in charge of the 'stun' waited above the pits for the propitious moment to knock them out … as soon as the animal fell to the ground … one of the sides of the box would open, at which point the animal that kept fighting, slid towards the slaughter chain" (Ricard, p. 81). Sue Coe[59] confirms that, "The cows are terrorized, put up resistance and kick raving mad," but if they stop,

---

58 Foer, J.S., *Eating Animals*, op. cit.

59 Coe, S., *Dead Meat*, New York, Four Walls Eight Windows, 1996. Coe's quotations are in Ricard; here pp. 88-89.

they are pushed with electric prods. A terrifying episode involves "a mare in labor in front of a fence. Two workers hit her while she gave birth to hurry her, then start the mother to slaughter and throw the baby into the scraps. The chief observes the scene indifferently, from an elevated corridor, his cowboy hat lowered over his head" (Ricard, p. 89). Horses don't enjoy a better destiny. As for chickens, in order to prevent them from hurting each other because of the stress, their beaks get regularly cut off without anesthesia, "with a guillotine equipped with heated blades … causing an unbearable pain." Quoting Foer, Ricard writes: "most of the male chicks are sucked in by a series of conductors and thrown on a powered plate … some end up shredded alive" (Ricard, p. 91). Among martyred animals there are also fishes and, even if they have no voice to scream their pain, "if we look carefully at an agonizing fish, his desperate efforts to breathe, his startled eyes and his last gasps tell you a lot about the torments he is undergoing …. When they are quickly recovered from the depths of the sea, decompression causes their swim bladder to burst, their eyes come out of their orbits, and the esophagus and stomach come out of their mouths" (Ricard, p. 118). Other animals who are victims of human cruelty are the geese for the *foie gras* and seals for their furs (Richard, pp. 122-123). There's a video of minks secretly recorded[60] that shows "a group of Chinese breeders who grab minks by their hind legs, twirl them in the air and then slam them violently to

---

60 Documentary by Mark Rissi, quoted by Ricard, p. 97, and in the note 42, p. 322.

the ground, then skin them alive, and after taking off all their fur, pile them into a stack on the side, and the skinners ... work and chat as if they were peeling zucchini, as if it was nothing, with a cigarette in their mouth."

"Unfortunately, these are not artfully edited horror scenes to exaggerate the reality. The numbers go beyond the unimaginable. Every year, more than one billion land animals are killed in France alone, more than 10 billions in the United States, and approximately 60 billions worldwide. China, India, and many other developing countries have recently stepped up industrial farming. In France, 95% of the pigs consumed comes from industrial farms. The same applies to 80% of laying hens and broiler chickens, and 90% of calves. As for the 40 millions rabbits killed each year, almost all of them are bred in cages" (Ricard, pp. 97-98). It's an international slaughter worthy of the globalization we hear so much about.

What we have just described with words is confirmed by the videos of the Casa Editrice AgireOra Edizioni and by investigations of national and international associations, Compassion in the World Farming (CIWF), and Essere Animali. The sites where you can find the documents are the following:

—https:/vimeo.com/album/53628389 for AGIREORA EDIZIONI
—info@ciwfonlus.it for CIWF
—www.essereanimali.org/cosa-facciamo/investigazioni/ for ESSERE ANIMALI

The scope of these references is to dissipate the ignorance on what happens to animals at the hands of humans, because the cruelty/ignorance combination is tragic. Ignorance is the contributing factor of such evil in the world. But in *Genesis* (2, 16-17) we read the ban to contrast it in God's commandment: "16: And the Lord God commanded the man 'you are free to eat from any tree in the garden; but you must not eat from the tree of knowledge of good and evil, for when you eat from it, you will certainly die." Homer, instead, in Dante's version reminds men, "Ye were not form'd to live the life of brutes, /But to pursue virtue and knowledge." (*Inferno*, Canto XXVI, trans. by Rev. H.F. Cary, London, Taylor and Hessey, 1819). In the Temple of Apollo at Delphi, men are reminded to "know themselves" so that they would avoid exceeding the limits of presumption and violence. And to Kant we owe the secular moral rule to be the norm to oneself (*Kritik der Praktischen Vernunft*). All this ancient and modern wisdom is long lost.

A ray of hope comes from Christian ethics where the irresponsible acts of humans against nature are discussed: Pontifex Franciscus in his encyclical *Laudato sì* holds that, "it is against human dignity to make animals suffer" (n. 130),[61] and a *vulnus*, a violation of rights, is denounced by Christian tradition.[62]

---

[61] As the *Catechismo della Chiesa Cattolica* "teaches", 2417, the Pope reminds us. Pontifex Franciscus, *Laudato sì. Sulla cura della Casa Comune.* Lettera Enciclica, Città del Vaticano, Libreria Editrice Vaticana, 2015, p. 87.

[62] Trianni, P., *Per un vegetarianesimo cristiano*, Padova, Edizioni Messaggero, 2017, p. 207.

This is a wound open from the legitimization of Anthropocentrism (*Genesis*, 1, 26-28), and is intensified by the "hell on earth of the industrial farming" and by the "tortures committed on animals."[63] It must be treated with a deep self-criticism and with a "fresh look," set up on an interior and adaptive dynamism.[64] In this way, it is hoped a "vegetarian conversion" of great courage and sensitivity that would "lead Christians to reconsider their life-style and diet,"[65] but that lay persons should reconsider them too. The wound in fact is in the conscience of those who tolerate the horrors of intensive farming and slaughterhouses and pretend not to know, while having all the tools to be informed. And once we know, it's impossible to "persevere in insensitivity and forever ignore the unspeakable sufferings that animals have to go through, only to please the gluttony."[66] We're all called upon in this vegetarian conversion.

---

63 *Idem*, p. 100.

64 *Idem*, pp. 109-124.

65 *Idem*, p. 101.

66 *Idem*, p. 98.

Q & A Session

If breeding was abolished, what would become of farmers?

They should convert to fruit and vegetable cultivation.

How would the great number of animals freed from intensive farming be managed?

With birth control.

Isn't the biological economy enough to improve the lives of the beasts now tortured in intensive farming?

No, because slaughterhouses would exist anyway and they are places of infinite suffering for animals.

Animals hunt and eat other animals: why shouldn't humans do the same thing?

If natural environments (forest lands and oceans for oil drilling) were not destroyed, animals would be able to manage and find their own balance that must be respected and not manipulated.

If the animals who provide wool, silk, leather were not killed anymore, what would we wear?

We would use other materials of plant origin or "cruelty free" products. Scientific research also is useful to discover other raw materials, eco-sustainable and without any animal constituents. Chemistry shows that it's possible for pharmaceuticals and cosmetics. The same thing can happen for clothing.

How to become vegetarians and/or vegans?

By putting one's hand on one's heart.

Bibliography

Angelino, G.P., Raggioli, A., *Consapevolezza negli animali,* Roma, Aracne Editrice, 2018

Arendt, H., *Eichmann in Jerusalem,* New York, Lotte Kohler, 1963. Quotations from the Italian edition: *La banalità del male. Eichmann a Gerusalemme,* Milano, Feltrinelli, 2016

Audet, J.N., Ducatez, S., Lefevre, L., "The Town Bird and the Country Bird," *Behavioral Ecology,* 2016, 27, pp. 637-644

Bentham, J., *An Introduction to the Principles of Morals and Legislation (1789),* Oxford, Clarendon Press, 1966

Bettiol, M., *Metafisica debole e razionalismo politico,* Napoli, ESI, 2002

Bono, G., De Mori, B., *Il confine superabile. Animali e qualità della vita,* Roma, Carrocci, 2011

Burch, R.L., Russell, W.L., *The principles of Human Experimental Technique,* UK, Wheathampstead, UTAW, 1992

Castiglione, S., Lombardi Vallauri, L., *La questione animale,* Milano, Giuffrè Editore, 2012

Cimatti, F., *Mente e linguaggio negli animali. Introduzione alla zoosemiotica cognitiva,* Roma, Carrocci, 1998

Coe, S., *Dead Meat,* New York, Four Walls Eight Windows, 1996

Cozzi, G., Gottardo, F., "Il nuovo sistema di allevamento del vitello a carne bianca," *Atti della Società di Buiatria,* vol. 37, 2005, pp. 441-454

Darwin, C., *On the Origin of Species,* London, John Murray, 1859

Descartes, R., *Discours de la méthode* (1637), quoted by Ditadi, G., *I filosofi e gli animali*

Ditadi, G., edited by, *I filosofi e gli animali,* Torino, Agire-Ora Edizioni, 2010

Dusi, E., "Quelle balene soffocate dal legame di famiglia," *La Repubblica,* March 24, 2018

European Convention for the Protection of Animals, ETS 125, Strasburg, 13.XI.1987

Foer, J.S., *Eating Animals,* New York, Little, Brown and Company, 2009. Quotation from the Italian edition: *Se niente importa,* Parma, Guanda Editore, 2013

Ford, H., *My Life and Work* (1922); (with Crowther) New York, Doubleday Page & Company, 1926

Gardiner, A., *Egyptian Grammar* (1927), Oxford, Griffith Institute, 1957

Gossen, H.H., *Die Entwicklung der Gesetze des menschlichen Verkers,* Berlin, Braunschweig, 1854

Isotta, P., *Il canto degli animali. I nostri fratelli e i loro sentimenti in musica e in poesia,* Venezia, Marsilio, 2017

Jevons, S.W., *Theory of Political Economy,* London, Macmillan, 1871

Leopardi, G., "Dialogo di Plotino e di Porfirio" in: *Operette Morali* (1835), Bari, Laterza, 1928

Logan, S.J., Sakata, J.T., "Vocal Motor Changes beyond the Sensitive Period for Song Plasticity", *Journal of Neurophysiology,* November 2014, pp. 2040-2052

Lymbery, P., Oakeshott, I., *Farmageddon. The True Cost of Cheap Meat,* London, Bloomsbury Publishing, 2014.

Quotations from the Italian edition: *Farmageddon. Il vero prezzo della carne economica*, Roma, Nutrimenti Sri, 2015

Mancuso, S., *Plant revolution. Le piante hanno* già *inventato il nostro futuro*, Firenze, Giunti, 2017

Marino, G.B., *Adone* (1623), Milano, Adelphi, 1988

Marshall, A., *Principles of Economics*, London, Macmillan, 1890

Menicali, S., *Introduzione al mondo animale*, ADIR-L'altro Diritto, *2009*

Ovidius, *Metamorphoses*, 3-8 A.D.

Patterson, C., *Eternal Treblinka: Our Treatment of Animals and the Holocaust*, New York, Lantern Books, 2002

Pellanda, A., "Dalla venerazione religiosa allo sfruttamento economico" in: *Noi e i diversi*, Atti del Convegno dell'Università di Padova 12/02/14, Padova, Padova University Press, 2014

Plutarchus, *De esu carnium (Of Eating Meat)*, 80-90 A.D. Italian translation edited by Ditadi, G., *Sul mangiar carne*, Torino, AgireOra Edizioni, 2016

Pontifex Franciscus, *Laudato sì. Sulla cura della casa comune*, Lettera Enciclica, Città del Vaticano, Libreria Editrice Vaticana, 2015

Regan, T., *The Case for Animals Rights*, Berkeley, University of California Press, 1983

Ricard, M., *Plaidoyer pour les animaux*, Paris, Allary Editions, 2014. Quotations from the Italian edition: *Sei un animale*, Trento, Sperling & Kupfer Editori, 2016

Rifkin, J., *Beyond Beef. The Rise and Fall of the Cattle Culture*, New York, Penguin Books, 1992. Quotations from the Italian edition: *Ecocidio. Ascesa e caduta della cultura della carne,* Milano, Mondadori, 2001

Ryder, R., *Victims of Science, The Use of Animals in Research,* London, Open Gate Press, 1983

Sinclair, U., *The Jungle,* New York, Double Day, 1906

Singer, P., *Animal Liberation,* New York, Harper Collins Publishers, 1975

Tallacchini, M., "Dignità, etica, science-based, democrazia: la tutela degli animali nella società europea della conoscenza" in: Chizzoniti, A.G., Tallaccchini, M., edited by, *Cibo e religioni. Diritto e Diritti,* Roma, Libellula Editore, 2010, pp. 297-322; Tallacchini, M., "Gli animali nella 'Società Europea della conoscenza': contraddizioni e prospettive," Università Cattolica del Sacro Cuore, *Pubblicatt,* 2015

Tassin, J., *Penser comme un arbre,* Paris, Odile Jacob, 2018

Theophrastus, *Peri Eusébeias (About Pity),* 316-315 B.C. Italian translation edited by Ditadi, G., *Della Pietà,* Este, Isonomia, 2005

Veblen, T., *The Theory of the Leisure Class* (1899), London, Allen & Unwin, 1924

Veronesi, U., Pappagallo, M., *Verso la scelta del vegetarismo. Il tumore si previene anche a tavola*, Milano, Giunti Editore, 2014

Websites

AgireOra Edizioni in:
   https://vimeo.com/album/5362838

Compassion In World Farming, Ciwf Italia in:
   info@ciwfonlus.it

Essere Animali in:
   www.essereanimali.org/cosa-facciamo/investigazioni/

Addendum

The Bat's Last Flight

In these dramatic times of Coronavirus, we have to wonder whether our inhuman cruelty to animals has turned against us. Simply put, this might be a case of "what goes around, comes around."

Human beings, proud of their scientific successes, and spoilt by their technological advances, thought they could shape the environment and animals to suit their own purposes. They converted the environment into a loft apartment, and animals into machines for the production of gastronomical delicacies.

They did not pause to think, not even after the first warning signs of disaster. When the ice packs began to melt, who cared about the bears and the seals? They could go and live somewhere else; they would adapt. When sea levels started to rise and threaten Venice, huge flood gates (perhaps MO.S.E., the Experimental Electromechanical Module?) would eventually come into operation, and the tourists would continue to flock to the city in their huge cruise ships. As the air became more and more polluted, the cars that were responsible could take them to breathe somewhere else during the holidays. Are the forests burning? Never mind, we can switch from producing timber to growing soybean, which will always be in great demand with all the animals to feed on the intensive breedings.

Ah yes, the animals! How could we give up eating tasty morsels of meat or roasting freshly-caught fish? The Chinese are planning to become the world's greatest "producers" of pigs, and to switch from being importers (of British sows) to exporters. Will they also start exporting (strictly live) bats for human consumption? Why not? It may be that Westerners enjoy eating them too in their race to consume material pleasures!

But this time the bats have fled the homunculus's plate to enter the immensity of the ether, and demonstrate how his extremely cruel and greedy consumption is taking humankind and the natural world to hell. Punishment for the criminal wickedness of humans against animals could only have come from the animals themselves, their innocent victims.

www.ingramcontent.com/pod-product-compliance
Lightning Source LLC
Chambersburg PA
CBHW052124110526
44592CB00013B/1734